Bike Trip

by BETSY and GIULIO MAESTRO

HarperCollins*Publishers*

For Barbara Fenton

Bike Trip
Text copyright © 1992 by Betsy Maestro
Illustrations copyright © 1992 by Giulio Maestro
Printed in the U.S.A. All rights reserved.
1   2   3   4   5   6   7   8   9   10
First Edition

Library of Congress Cataloging-in-Publication Data
Maestro, Betsy.
  Bike trip / by Betsy and Giulio Maestro.
  Summary: A family takes a bicycle trip and experiences the
sights, sounds, and smells of town, country, and seashore.
  ISBN 0-06-022731-1. — ISBN 0-06-022732-X (lib. bdg.)
  1. Cycling—Juvenile literature.   2. Cycling—Safety
measures—Juvenile literature.   3. Bicycle touring—Juvenile
literature.   [1. Bicycles and bicycling.]   I. Maestro, Giulio.
II. Title.
GV1043.5.M34   1992   90-35935
796.6—dc20   CIP
                                                    AC

Today's the day! We're taking a bike trip into town. There's a lot to do before we go. I fill the water bottles and Mom packs our tool kit. Dad puts my new odometer on my bike. "It's all set, Josh. Now you'll know how many miles you've gone."

Before we get on our bikes, we try out the brakes and check the tires for air. My rear tire seems a little low, so I pump it up till it's just right. We all put on our helmets. I love mine. It's bright yellow with real racing stripes on it.

We walk our bikes to the end of the driveway and stop to check for traffic. When the road is clear, I shout, "Okay, let's go!" We ride out one by one with me in the lead. My sister, Beth, has her own seat on the back of Dad's bike.

We ride along in the same direction as the traffic, close to the right-hand side of the road. It's a narrow road, so we have to leave room for cars to go by. We watch out for branches and big stones near the edge. We ride single file, and not too close together, in case we have to stop suddenly.

It's so quiet. All I can hear is the wind whistling gently past my face and the whirring of my tires on the blacktop. Now and then we hear a car coming. The sound gets closer and closer and then fades away again as the car passes us and moves out of sight.

We pedal by a large farm with horses grazing in a field. They lift their heads as we pass. I can hear cows mooing in a nearby pasture. There is a sweet smell of grass and hay. It tickles my nose a bit, and I sneeze!

I love going really fast on my bike, but now I pedal along more slowly and look around. I never see this much from in the car.

The road begins to get narrower as we come to a railroad bridge. "Slow down, Josh!" shouts Mom. I squeeze my handbrakes, and my bike slows to a stop. The wooden bridge makes a clackety, hollow sound as we walk our bikes across.

There are no trains coming and you can see a long stretch of track in both directions. Some workers are fixing the track just below. We watch them for a few minutes before we ride on.

About two miles down the road we come to a busy crossing. Trucks and cars zoom by, and we have to wait. "Wave at this truck," I shout to Beth. We both wave, and the truck driver gives us a loud blast of his horns.

We walk our bikes across as soon as there's a break in the traffic. Now I check my odometer. "We've already gone six miles!"

"Great!" says Dad. "Only two more miles!"

When we get into town, the sidewalks are filled with people. There's a big art show today, and there are pictures everywhere.

"Let's stop and look around," says Mom. So we lock up our bikes and start to explore.

There are some bright paintings of sailboats and a painting of cows just like the ones we saw today. At a booth there are some tiny, hand-carved animals for sale. I pick out a little duck, and my sister gets a sleeping kitten.

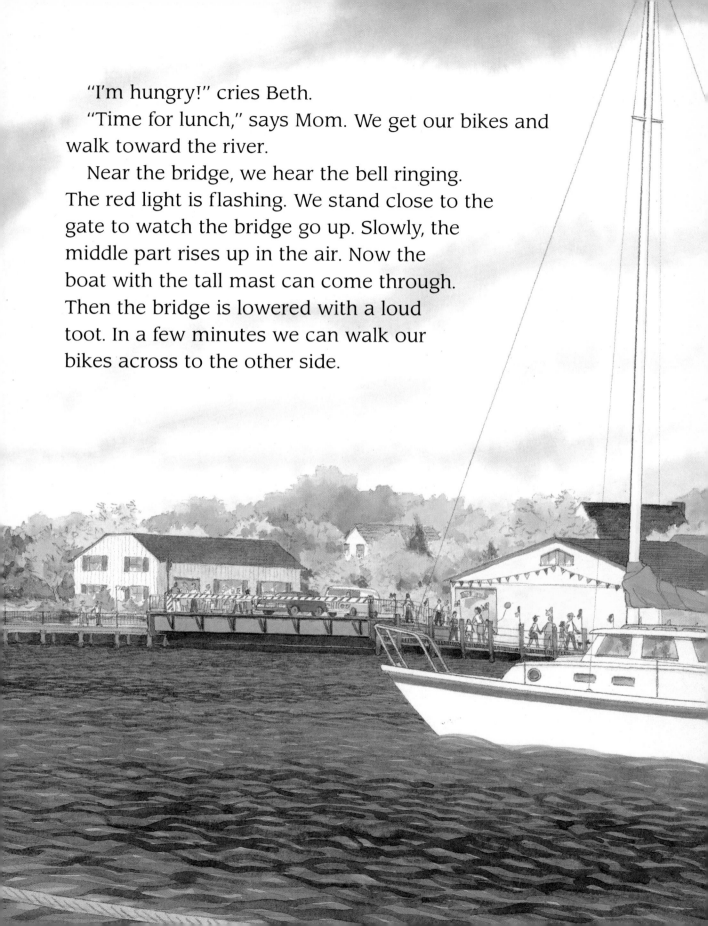

"I'm hungry!" cries Beth.

"Time for lunch," says Mom. We get our bikes and walk toward the river.

Near the bridge, we hear the bell ringing. The red light is flashing. We stand close to the gate to watch the bridge go up. Slowly, the middle part rises up in the air. Now the boat with the tall mast can come through. Then the bridge is lowered with a loud toot. In a few minutes we can walk our bikes across to the other side.

We find a restaurant where we can have lunch right by the river. After the waitress takes our order, Dad pulls out our road map. He shows me just where we are and the route we will follow after lunch.

When my lunch comes I gobble it down. I was really hungry and thirsty, after all that pedaling! Then we get ice cream cones and walk down to see the ducks.

After we've rested awhile, we ride out of town. We're taking a different route going back. Mom's in the lead now, and she puts her left hand out to signal for a left turn. Dad and I follow along, and after a few more turns we're on another small, quiet road.

I can tell we're near the water by the salty smell in the air. There's tall marsh grass all around us, and up ahead is a small tidal river. The tide is low, and we stop to watch tiny crabs darting in and out of holes in the mud.

"Look at all those turtles!" Dad calls out, pointing to a large rock in the river. "They're sunning themselves."

We turn away from the water and soon come to a steep hill. I have to stand up on my pedals and push really hard to make it to the top. Mom and Dad can change gears on their bikes so it's easier to pedal uphill.

I love the feeling of speed when I coast down the other side. My brakes are on the whole time, but I still feel like I'm really flying! The going down part is always over too soon.

Up ahead where the train tracks go over the road I
see an underpass. Underneath, it is as cool and dark as
a cave. I shout, "Hello," so I can hear my echo. Just as
we come out into the sun, a passenger train roars by.
What a noise! Beth covers her ears.

It's hot, and we all need a little rest. Except for my sister. She hasn't had to do any work at all! We pull over to a shady spot. I check my odometer again. "Guess what, we've already gone fourteen miles today," I tell everyone.

I push my kickstand down and leave my bike standing in the dirt. We all sit in the cool grass. I'm so thirsty! The water in my bottle isn't cold anymore, but I don't care.

On the way home we stop at the farm market. I help pick out some corn and lettuce and berries for our dinner. We just manage to fit them all into our basket and bike bags.

"Only one more mile to go," says Mom as we pedal out. My legs are getting a little tired, but I know I can do one more mile.

NATIVE BUTTER AND SUGAR CORN

We're home! We pull into our driveway and put our bikes away in the garage. My legs feel rubbery when I walk. I guess they're not used to pedaling sixteen miles! That's the most I've ever done. Now I'm starving!

When we sit down for dinner, everyone starts to talk at once. "What a great time!" "Let's do it again!" "I had fun!" "Maybe next weekend…"
  I can't wait!

If you and your family take a bike trip, here are some rules you should follow:

1. Always **keep to the right.** Ride with the traffic.
2. **Ride single file.** Stay out of the way of faster car traffic.
3. **Don't swerve or weave or switch lanes.** Try to travel in a straight line close to the edge of the road.
4. **Obey all traffic rules.** Bicyclists must stop for stop signs and obey traffic signals.
5. **Stop at intersections.** Look both ways before you cross or turn.
6. **Use hand signals.** Use the signals shown on this page when you turn or stop.
7. **Watch out for pedestrians.** People on foot have the right of way.
8. **Don't overload your bike.** Never ride double or carry a heavy load. Small children should be carried in proper carriers.
9. **Don't do tricks.** Always ride with your hands on the handlebars. The road is not a safe place for tricks or stunts.
10. **Keep your bike in good shape.** Make sure everything on your bike is in working order. Check your brakes and tires before each ride.
11. **Be alert.** Watch for possible dangers, such as rocks in the road, dogs, large puddles, or glass.
12. If you can, **wear a helmet.** In an accident, it will protect your head from serious injury.
13. **Use a headlamp and reflectors** for night riding. Wear light colors.
14. **Wear bright clothes** for daytime rides.
15. **Avoid sharp turns,** particularly on dirt, gravel, or sand.

Signals

Left turn:
left arm straight out

Right turn:
left arm bent at elbow,
with hand pointing up.

Stopping or slowing down:
left arm held away from body,
out and pointing down.

Have fun!